S0-EFO-122

Love
Lines

Vern
McLellan

HARVEST HOUSE PUBLISHERS
Eugene, Oregon 97402

Unless otherwise indicated, all Scripture quotations in this book are taken from The Living Bible, Copyright © 1971 owned by assignment by Illinois Regional Bank N.A. (as trustee). Used by permission of Tyndale House Publishers, Inc., Wheaton, Illinois 60189. All rights reserved.

Verses marked KJV are taken from the King James Version of the Bible.

Verses marked NKJV are taken from the New King James Version, Copyright © 1979, 1980, 1982 by Thomas Nelson, Inc., Publishers. Used by permission.

Illustrations by Sandy Silverthorne

LOVE LINES

Copyright © 1990 by Vern McLellan
Published by Harvest House Publishers
Eugene, Oregon 97402

Library of Congress Cataloging-in-Publication Data

McLellan, Vernon K.
    Love lines: a lighthearted look at love & romance /
by Vern McLellan.
    ISBN 0-89081-820-7
    1. Love—Humor.   2. Love—Quotations, maxims, etc.
    I. Title.
PN6231.L6M38   1990.
081—dc20   89-71634
                                              CIP

Printed in the United States of America.

Dedicated to my wife, Mary,
the love of my life

Contents

American humorist Will Rogers once said, "We are all here for a spell; get all the good laughs you can." That's what I've tried to do in the pages of *Love Lines*.

Included are smiles, put-downs, and witticisms that will encourage you to:

- *joke about all the stages of love*—from friendship to senior expressions of love—so you won't take life too seriously.

- *stoke the fires of romantic communication.* In this book you will notice ideas and strategies that, though humorously stated, will help you build a stronger love-life.

- *seek a better understanding of wedlock.* You'll discover, directly and indirectly, keys to unlocking deadlocks in your love relationships.

- *invoke God's help and leadership in your marriage.*

- *smoke out* suspicion, doubt, and distrust in all areas of loving relationships.

- *give wisdom and common sense high priority* in your love-life.

May the principles and pointers in *Love Lines* enrich your relationships in the vast area of love.

—Vern McLellan
Charlotte, North Carolina

Friendship

A friend is one who knows all about you and still loves you just the same.

Did you hear about the two janitors in a large office building? They were broom mates; they even swept together; in fact they were dust inseparable.

— 🐛 —

He who seeks friends without faults stays forever without friends.

— 🐛 —

Chance makes our parents, but choice makes our friends—Delille.

— 🐛 —

Friends are people who stick together until debt do them part.

— 🐛 —

A friend doubles a man's joy and cuts his sorrow in half—Bacon.

A friend is one who knows all about you and still loves you just the same.

— 🐛 —

Real friends are those who, when you've made a fool of yourself, don't feel that you've done a permanent job.

— 🐛 —

The best way to keep a friend is not to give him away.

— 🐛 —

The world needs more warm hearts and fewer hot heads.

— 🐛 —

The best vitamin for developing a friendship is B-1.

— 🐛 —

A friend is a person who goes around saying nice things about you behind your back.

— 🐛 —

The reason a dog is man's best friend is because he does not pretend; he proves it.

Nothing in the world is friendlier than a wet dog.

— ❧ —

Prosperity begets friends; adversity proves them.

— ❧ —

A friend is one before whom I may think aloud—Emerson.

— ❧ —

True friends are like diamonds,
  Precious but rare;
False friends are like autumn leaves,
  Found everywhere.

— ❧ —

Never explain—your friends do not need it, and your enemies will not believe it anyway.

— ❧ —

He who has many friends is not caught by darkness in the road.

— ❧ —

The best way to wipe out a friendship is to sponge on it.

To have friends we must be friendly. Friendliness is a matter of being someone...more than it is doing something—Swindoll.

Friends are like fiddle strings—they must not be screwed too tightly.

There are "friends" who pretend to be friends, but there is a friend who sticks closer than a brother—Proverbs 18:24.

Love Is a Many Splendored Thing

Love's great desire is to give.

Love is oceans of emotions entirely surrounded by expanses of expenses.

Love is said to be blind, but I know lots of fellows in love who can see twice as much in their sweethearts as I can—Billings.

Love is a form of insanity which makes a girl marry her boss and work for him the rest of her life without salary.

Did you hear about the nearsighted turtle that fell in love with an army helmet?

All the world loves a lover.

Love, like a spring rain, is pretty hard to be in the middle of without getting some on you—The Country Parson.

— ❦ —

The love we give away is the only love we keep —Hubbard.

— ❦ —

Love's great desire is to give.

— ❦ —

Someday, after we have mastered the winds, the waves, the tides, gravity, and outer space, we will harness the energies of love: And then, for the second time in the history of the world, man will have discovered fire.

— ❦ —

Ironic, isn't it, that in tennis, "love" is nothing, but in life, "love" is everything!

— ❦ —

Love makes the lonelies go away.

— ❦ —

Make love your number-one aim. Love is your greatest possibility in the one life you have to live.

There's no love like the first love.

— 🐌 —

You can give without loving but you can't love without giving—Carmichael.

— 🐌 —

A practical nurse is one who falls in love with a wealthy patient.

— 🐌 —

A bell is not a bell until you ring it;
    A song is not a song until you sing it.
Love in your heart is not put there to stay;
    Love is not love until you give it away.

— 🐌 —

Love is...

    Slow to suspect—quick to trust.
    Slow to condemn—quick to justify.
    Slow to offend—quick to defend.
    Slow to expose—quick to shield.
    Slow to reprimand—quick to forbear.
    Slow to belittle—quick to appreciate.
    Slow to demand—quick to give.
    Slow to provoke—quick conciliate.
    Slow to hinder—quick to help.
    Slow to resent—quick to forgive.

Love will find a way!

— ❧ —

There's no love like the first love.

— ❧ —

Love is very patient and kind, never jealous or envious, never boastful or proud, never haughty or selfish or rude. Love does not demand its own way. It is not irritable or touchy. It does not hold grudges and will hardly even notice when others do it wrong. It is never glad about injustice, but rejoices whenever truth wins out. If you love someone you will be loyal to him no matter what the cost. You will always believe in him, always expect the best of him, and always stand your ground in defending him.

All the special gifts and powers from God will someday come to an end, but love goes on forever (1 Corinthians 13:4-8).

— ❧ —

A lovelorn porcupine was taking an evening stroll when he bumped into a cactus. "Is that you, sweetheart?" he asked tenderly.

— ❧ —

The biggest drawback to budding love is that it leads to a lot of blooming expense.

Love is the basic need of human nature, for without it, life is disrupted—emotionally, mentally, spiritually, and physically—Dr. Karl Menninger.

— 🍎 —

'Tis better to have loved and lost than never to have loved at all—Tennyson.

— 🍎 —

How far you go in life depends on your being tender with the young, compassionate with the aged, sympathetic with the striving, and tolerant of the weak and the strong because someday in life you will have been all of these—George Washington Carver.

— 🍎 —

Love is the medicine for the sickness of mankind. We can live if we have love—Dr. Karl Menninger.

— 🍎 —

Love has been described as a five-ring circus: First comes the telephone ring; then the engagement ring; then the wedding ring; then the teething ring; and after that, the suffer-ring.

— 🍎 —

Love begins when a person feels another person's needs are as important as his own—Sullivan.

Love is only for the young, the middle-aged, and the old.

The greatest happiness of life is the conviction that we are loved—loved for ourselves, or rather, in spite of ourselves—Victor Hugo.

Love is the only fire against which there is no insurance.

Love is woman's eternal spring and man's eternal fall—Helen Rowland.

— ❦ —

Love is an itch around the heart that's impossible to scratch.

— ❦ —

Love seeketh not itself to please,
   Nor for itself hath any care,
But for another gives its ease,
   And builds a heaven in hell's despair.

— ❦ —

Teacher: And so you see, children, love is the one thing you can give in abundance and still have plenty left.

Jimmy: How about measles?

— ❦ —

Love is an irresistible desire to be irresistibly desired—Robert Frost.

— ❦ —

Love is the triumph of the imagination over intelligence—H.L. Mencken.

Love is the thing that enables a woman to smile while she mops up the floor after her husband has walked across it in his muddy boots.

— 🐛 —

Love is blind—and marriage is an eye-opener.

— 🐛 —

Better to have loved a short man than never to have loved a tall.

— 🐛 —

Love beats its tattoo on every lover's pocketbook.

— 🐛 —

Did you hear about the fellow who wore his girl's picture in his watch because he thought he would learn to love her in time?

— 🐛 —

When a woman loves a man, he can make her do anything she wants to do.

— 🐛 —

We are shaped and fashioned by what we love—Goethe.

Passion is an emotion; love is a choice.

— ❧ —

Respect is what we owe; love, what we give
—Bailey.

— ❧ —

To love and win is the best thing; to love and lose
the next best—Thackeray.

— ❧ —

Tomcat: My wonderful one, I would die for you.

Pussycat: Yeah, but how many times?

— ❧ —

God has given to man a short time here upon
earth, and yet upon this short time eternity
depends—Jeremy Taylor.

— ❧ —

What you keep to yourself, you lose; what you
give away, you keep forever.

— ❧ —

Love is the feeling that makes a woman make a
man make a fool of himself.

Love cures people—both the ones who give it and the ones who receive it—Dr. Karl Menninger.

— 🍎 —

Life is just one fool thing after another; love is just two fool things after each other.

— 🍎 —

Love must be learned, and learned again and again; there is no end to it. Hate needs no instruction, but wants only to be provoked —Katherine Ann Porter.

— 🍎 —

She: Do you love me, Herman?
He: Yes!
She: Would you die for me?
He: No, mine is an undying love.

— 🍎 —

Love is like the measles; we all have to go through it—Jerome K. Jerome.

— 🍎 —

It is possible that a man can be so changed by love as hardly to be recognized as the same person—Terence.

A bright eye indicates curiosity; a black eye, too much.

In life, actions speak louder than words, but in love, the eyes do—Susan B. Anthony.

Not a day passes that I have not loved you. Not one night that I have not clasped you in my arms—Napoleon to Josephine.

Love is a blindness that owes its prevalence to the sense of touch.

Love is a fruit in season at all times, and within the reach of every hand—Mother Teresa of Calcutta.

Love does not dominate; it cultivates—Goethe.

Love is a passion fancy.

Love is the last word in a telegram.

The glory of life is to love, not to be loved; to give, not to get; to serve, not to be served. Love is the true miracle, and to the one who loves comes both wonder and joy—Hugh Black.

Through the eyes of love you see your mate as alert rather than nosy, thrifty rather than stingy, expressive rather than too talkative, sensitive rather than touchy, confident rather than cocky.

Love betters what is best.

Love without return is like a question without an answer.

Some persons, by hating vice too much, come to love men too little.

God is love. Love knows no limits.

Mother-love is ever in its spring.

There's a wideness in God's mercy like the
wideness of the sea,
There is kindness in His justice which is more
than liberty.
For the love of God is broader than the measure
of man's mind,
And the heart of the Eternal is most wonderfully
kind.

—Frederick W. Faber

There is no fear in love; but perfect love casteth
out fear—1 John 4:18 KJV.

Greater love hath no man than this, that a man
lay down his life for his friends—John 15:13 KJV.

Love's night is noon.

Love is the affection that enables a woman to
forgive her husband for forgetting her birthday but
remembering her age.

Love levels all inequalities.

If you would be loved, love and be lovable
—Franklin.

The only victory over love is flight—Napoleon.

Everybody in love is blind.

Love is blind, but the neighbors ain't!

Love's fire, if it once goes out, is hard to rekindle.

The spectrum of love, as St. Paul shows it to us, contains nine component parts: patience; kindness; generosity; humility; courtesy; unselfishness; good temper; lack of suspicion; sincerity—Preston Bradley.

Respect is love in plainclothes—Byrne.

Paradise is always where love dwells.

The mystery and magnificence of love is that two people can become one and yet remain two.

— 🍎 —

The way to love anything is to realize that it might be lost—Chesterton.

— 🍎 —

The great tragedy of life is not that men perish, but that they cease to love—Maugham.

— 🍎 —

Love is a spendthrift, leaves its arithmetic at home, is always "in the red"—Paul Scherer.

— 🍎 —

The greatest love is a mother's; then comes a dog's; then a sweetheart's—Polish proverb.

— 🍎 —

Love is what you've been through with somebody.

— 🍎 —

Love is a softening of the hearteries.

— 🍎 —

It is hard to express love with a clenched fist.

The sunlight of love will kill all the germs of jealousy and hate.

— 🍎 —

Money will buy a fine dog, but only love will make him wag his tail.

— 🍎 —

Where love resides, God abides.

— 🍎 —

Unfortunately, it is easy to imagine that anyone hates you, and hard to think anyone loves you. But you must be bold to believe in love if you would be happy—Dr. Frank Crane.

— 🍎 —

It is nice to feel the atmosphere of love round you once in a while, and nobody out of tune—Woodberry.

— 🍎 —

Love does not recognize the difference between peasant and mikado—Japanese proverb.

— 🍎 —

Love is like butter, it goes well with bread—Yiddish proverb.

When a woman likes to wait on a man, that settles it: She loves him—E.W. Howe.

— 🐛 —

Love quickens all the senses—except common sense.

— 🐛 —

Love looks through a telescope; envy, through a microscope.

— 🐛 —

Love is a fabric which never fades, no matter how often it is washed in the water of adversity and grief.

— 🐛 —

Love is the glue that cements friendship; jealousy keeps it from sticking.

— 🐛 —

Love is like a vaccination—when it takes hold, you don't have to be told.

— 🐛 —

Love is an unusual game; there are either two winners or none.

Love is a condition of the mind at a time when the mind is out of condition.

One of the tragedies of American life is that love is being defined by those who have experienced so little of it.

When you hear bells ringing, feel butterflies fluttering, and act as though you have bees in your bonnet—that's real love!

Love seeks not limits, but outlets.

The course of true love never runs smoothly—and the detours aren't much better.

This will be a better world when the power of love replaces the love of power.

Love may not make the world go around, but it sure makes the trip worthwhile.

The loneliest place in the world is the human heart when love is absent—McKenzie.

It is love that asks, that seeks, that knocks, that finds, and that is faithful to what it finds
—St. Augustine.

— ❦ —

Love is a season's pass on the shuttle between heaven and hell—Don Dickerman.

— ❦ —

Love is perpetual emotion.

— ❦ —

I never knew a night so black
   Light failed to follow in its track.
I never knew a storm so gray
   It never failed to have its clearing day.
I never knew such bleak despair
   that there was not a right somewhere.
I never knew an hour so drear
   Love could not fill it full of cheer.
              —John Kendrick Bangs

— ❦ —

He prayeth best, who loveth best,
   All things both great and small;
For the dear God who loveth us,
   He made and loveth all.
              —Coleridge

Money cannot buy love, but it makes shopping for it a lot easier.

— 🍎 —

As soon as you cannot stay away from a woman, you love her.

— 🍎 —

Love demands all, and has a right to it —Beethoven.

— 🍎 —

Love and eggs are best when they are fresh— Russian proverb.

— 🍎 —

Try to reason about love and you will lose your reason—French proverb.

— 🍎 —

Perfect love sometimes does not come 'til the first grandchild—Welsh proverb.

— 🍎 —

In expressing love, we belong among the underdeveloped countries.

A woman unsatisfied must have luxuries. But a woman who loves a man would sleep on a board— D.H. Lawrence.

Faults are thick where love is thin—James Howell.

One of our greatest learning tasks is how to give and receive love.

I have learned that only two things are necessary to keep one's wife happy. First, let her think she is having her own way. And second, let her have it— Lyndon B. Johnson.

The magic of first love is our ignorance that it can ever end—Disraeli.

The pains of love be sweeter far
Than all other pleasures are—Dryden.

Love is a heartburn, a heart attack.

Tell me whom you love, and I will tell you what you are—Houssaye.

— ❦ —

Love is not altogether a delirium, yet it has many points in common therewith—Carlyle.

— ❦ —

Love will find a way. Indifference will find an excuse.

— ❦ —

Light love, heavy consequences.

— ❦ —

Where love is, no room is too small.

— ❦ —

Lovers always think that other people have had their eyes put out—Spanish proverb.

— ❦ —

Love makes the world go 'round.

— ❦ —

Works, and not words, are the proof of love.

Love makes all hard hearts gentle—Herbert.

Did you hear about the young man who loved a girl so much he worshiped the very ground her father discovered oil on?

How Do I Love Thee?

How do I love thee? Let me count the ways.
I love thee to the depth and breadth and
  height
My soul can reach, when feeling out of sight
For the ends of Being and ideal Grace.
I love thee to the level of every day's
Most quiet need, by sun and candle-light.
I love thee freely, as men strive for Right;
I love thee purely, as men turn from Praise.
I love thee with the passion put to use
In my old griefs, and with my childhood's
  faith.
I love thee with a love I seemed to lose
With my lost saints, I love thee with the
  breath,
Smiles, tears, of all my life! and, if God
  choose,
I shall but love thee better after death.

—Elizabeth Barrett Browning

Affection

In spite of all his faults, there is no creature worthier of affection than man.

—Goethe

The young desperately crave physical affection. Howard Maxwell of Los Angeles is a man in tune with his times. So when his four-year-old daughter, Melinda, acquired a fixation for *The Three Little Pigs* and demanded that he read it to her night after night, Maxwell, very pleased with himself, tape-recorded the story.

When Melinda next asked for it, he simply switched on the playback.

This worked for a couple of nights, but then one evening Melinda pushed the storybook at her father.

"Now, honey," he said, "you know how to turn on the recorder."

"Yes," said Melinda, "but I can't sit on its lap."

— ❧ —

Caresses, expressions of one sort or another, are necessary to the life of the affections as leaves are to the life of the tree. If they are wholly restrained, love will die at the roots.

Above all else, guard your affections. For they influence everything else in your life—Proverbs 4:23.

— —

A hug is a roundabout way of expressing affection.

— —

If you wish to gain affection, bestow it—Seneca.

— —

We may not return the affection of those who like us, but we always respect their good judgment.

— —

In spite of all his faults, there is no creature worthier of affection than man—Goethe.

— —

As the rolling stone gathers no moss, so the roving heart gathers no affection—Jameson.

— —

Dating

The biggest worry of a doting father is usually a dating daughter.

A girl's idea of happiness is being pursued by the guy she's chasing.

— ❦ —

When a guy goes nuts about a gal he must start shelling out.

— ❦ —

Guy: Do you have a good after-shave lotion?

Clerk: Yes, here's one that will drive your girlfriend crazy. It smells like a new car.

— ❦ —

Until a boy is 16 he's a boy scout; after that he's a girl scout.

— ❦ —

Girls who go with punks should expect fireworks.

He: May I hold your hand?

She: It isn't very heavy. I think I can manage it, thank you.

— 🐛 —

Some girls break a date just by going out with him.

— 🐛 —

The second time he asked her out
　　Her "No!" was definite and stout.
His conversation themes, you see,
　　Were chiefly I, myself, and me.

— 🐛 —

The young man walked over to the counter where the greeting cards were being sold.

"Do you have anything sentimental?" he asked.

"We certainly do," replied the clerk. "Here's one that says 'To the only girl I've ever loved'."

"Great!" came the reply. "Let me have seven of them."

— 🐛 —

"Where was your big brother going with that bag of oats?"

"Taking his girl out to dinner. He says she eats like a horse."

"Their going steady is a secret."
"So everybody says."

Flirting

My love is gone,
Him did me dirt.
Me never knew
Him was a flirt.
To those who love
Let I forbid,
Lest they be dood
Like I been did.

Flirting: wishful winking.

There once was a man not unique
Who imagined himself quite a sheik.
But the girls didn't fall
For the fella at all....
He only made 20 a week.

The biggest worry of a doting father is usually a dating daughter.

They strolled down the lane together,
   The sky was studded with stars.
They reached the gate in silence,
   And he lifted up the bars.
She neither smiled nor thanked him,
   For indeed she knew not how.
For he was just a farmer boy,
   And she—a Jersey cow.

Valentine

I shot an arrow into the air
It fell to earth I know not where.
It pierced the heart of a girl I knew,
And now I'm stuck and she is, too.

When Cupid aims for the mark, he usually
Mrs. it.

— ❦ —

It's the glancing shot by Cupid, the one that
barely nicks you, that causes the most suffering.

— ❦ —

There is evidence that Cupid is a trapper as well
as a hunter.

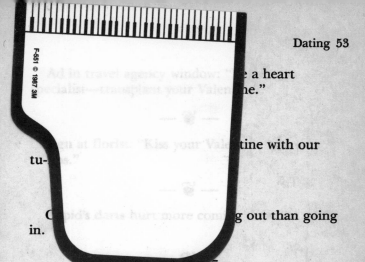

Ad in travel agency window: "Be a heart specialist—transplant your Valentine."

— ❦ —

Sign at florist: "Kiss your Valentine with our tu-lips."

— ❦ —

Cupid's darts hurt more coming out than going in.

Ted: I hear Cupid almost got you last week.
Fred: Yes, I had an arrow escape.

Pam: Guys are all alike.
Tam: Guys are all I like, too.

Girl: Whenever I look at you, I'm reminded of a famous man.
Boy: You flatter me. Who was the man?
Girl: Darwin.

— ❦ —

The two kinds of wood that make a match: he would and she would.

Tom: Meet me at the Waldorf-Astoria at eight.
Sue: The Waldorf? Say, that's a nice place.
Tom: Yea, and it's close to where we're going,
   too.

"If you refuse to go out with me," said the boy with intensity, "I shall die."

She refused.

Eighty-five years later he died.

— ❦ —

"You will have a happier life," a father warned his pretty daughter, "if you avoid trying to convert a *boy*friend into a *buy* friend."

— ❦ —

A girl met an old boyfriend at a party, and she decided to be a little sarcastic.

"Sorry," she murmured when the hostess introduced him to her, "I didn't get your name."

"I know you didn't," replied the ex-boyfriend, "but you certainly tried hard enough."

— ❦ —

Two boys were playing marbles together when a very pretty little girl walked by.

One boy stopped and said to his pal, "Boy, when I stop hating girls, she's the one I'm going to stop hating first!"

— ❦ —

Two brothers wanted to ask a favor of their mother.

"You ask her," said the older brother.

"No," said the younger brother. "You ask her. You've known her longer than I have."

Cal: Why does a girl say she's been shopping when she hasn't bought a thing?

Sal: For the same reason a boy says he's been fishing.

— 🐛 —

Two high school boys were chatting during football practice:

"Debbie sure is a smart girl," remarked one to the other. "She has brains enough for two."

"Then she's just the girl for you," said the other.

— 🐛 —

Father: How dare you! What do you mean by hugging my daughter?

Boy: "I—I—I was just carrying out the biblical injunction, 'Hold fast that which is good.' "

— 🐛 —

Boy: I would like to marry you.

Girl: Well, leave your name and address and if nothing better turns up, I'll notify you.

— 🐛 —

Boy: You could learn to love me, couldn't you?

Girl: Well, I learned to eat spinach.

— 🐛 —

Saying no to a guy: I'm sorry, I can't see you Sunday. I'm expecting a headache.

"Is your girlfriend having any success in learning how to drive?"

"Well, the road is beginning to turn when she does."

— ❦ —

Boy problem: I'll either have to get a smaller car or take out a smaller girl.

— ❦ —

Mother: Your boyfriend's car is at the door.
Daughter: I know, I hear it knocking.

— ❦ —

Girl driver (breathless after narrow escape): I had the right of way, didn't I?
Boyfriend: You did. But the other fellow had the truck.

— ❦ —

"Son, did you use the car last night?"
"Yes, Dad. I took some of the boys for a ride."
"Well, tell them I found two of their lipsticks."

— ❦ —

Teenage love—a feeling you feel when you feel that what you feel is a feeling you never felt before.

Did you hear about the dumb girl who turned a deaf ear to a blind date?

The tired old jalopy chugged up to the toll bridge.

"Half a dollar," said the bridge tender.

"Sold," said the boy driver.

THE TEEN COMMANDMENTS
by a teenager for teenagers

1. Don't let your parents down; they brought you up.
2. Be smart, obey. You'll give orders yourself someday.
3. Ditch dirty thoughts fast, or they'll ditch you.
4. Stop and think before you drink.
5. Show-off driving is juvenile; don't act your age.
6. Pick your friends wisely. You become what they are.
7. Choose a date fit for a mate.
8. Don't go steady unless you're ready.
9. Love God and neighbor.
10. Live carefully. The soul you save may be your own.

Solomon said, "Remember now your Creator in the days of your youth"   —Ecclesiastes 12:1 NKJV.

Did you hear about the girl who always flirts with the rookie butcher? She's playing for bigger steaks.

— 🍎 —

No wonder it's tough to be a teenager: Half the adults tell him to "find himself" and the other half are telling him to "get lost."

— 🍎 —

Why can't life's problems hit us when we're 17 and know all the answers?

— 🍎 —

Father (to teenage daughter): I want you home by 11 o'clock.
Daughter: But, Daddy, I am no longer a child!
Father: I know. That's why I want you home by 11.

— 🍎 —

A generation crisis in reverse occurred when a teenager drove his car into the garage and ran over his father's bicycle.

— 🍎 —

Teenager to doctor listening to her heart: Does it sound broken?

Teenager: Father, when I get through college, I've decided I'm going to settle down and raise chickens.

Father: Son, take my advice. Forget about the chickens and raise owls. Their hours will suit you better.

If little Red Riding Hood lived today,
  The modern girl would scorn her.
She only had to meet one wolf,
  Not one on every corner.

A teenage girl is someone who will scream at a mouse, and smile at a wolf.

Kissing

A kiss is the shortest distance between two.

Young lady, be wary of Cupid
   And list to the lines of this verse.
To let a fool kiss you is stupid
   But to let a kiss fool you is worse.

— ❧ —

She: Am I the first girl you ever kissed?
He: Now that you mention it, you do look
familiar.

— ❧ —

Boy: I want to be honest. You're not the first girl
I've ever kissed.
Girl: I want to be honest. You've got a lot to
learn.

— ❧ —

Boy: Then she kissed me and I knew it was
puppy love. Her nose was cold.

Puppy love leads to a dog's life.

He's kissed so many girls, he could do it with his eyes closed.

Confession

Steven kissed me in the spring,
Robert in the fall,
But Carson only looked at me
And never kissed at all.

Steven's kiss was lost in jest,
Robert's lost in play.
But the kiss in Carson's eyes
Haunts me night and day.

Did you hear about the student trombone player who kissed his girlfriend and blew her brains out?

Kiss me, baby—nothing makes me sick.

Question: How do porcupines make love?
Answer: Very carefully.

He: How about a kiss?
She: Sorry, sir, but I have scruples.
He: That's okay. I've been vaccinated.

— 🍒 —

One teenage girl to another: He hasn't really kissed me yet, but he steamed my glasses a couple of times.

— 🍒 —

Did you know that high heels were invented by a girl who got tired of being kissed on the forehead?

— 🍒 —

He was a bit shy, and after she had thrown her arms around him for bringing her a bouquet of flowers, he started to leave.

"I'm sorry I offended you," she said to him.

"Oh, I'm not offended," he replied. "I'm going for more flowers."

— 🍒 —

Boy Eskimo: Dearest, I pushed my dog team 100 miles through ice and snow today to see you and tell you I love you.

Girl Eskimo: Aw, that's a lot of mush.

— 🍒 —

Then there was the absentminded professor who kissed the door and slammed his wife.

Before I heard professors tell
   The facts about a kiss,
I had considered kissing you
   The closest thing to bliss.

But now I know biology
   And sit and sigh and moan.
Six thousand small bacteria
   And I thought we were alone.

— ❦ —

Did you hear about the girl with the gleam in her eye? Someone bumped her elbow while she was brushing her teeth.

— ❦ —

A kiss that speaks volumes is seldom a first edition.

— ❦ —

George: She looks at me as a brother. Every time I kiss her, she yells, "Oh, brother!"

— ❦ —

A kiss over the phone is like a straw hat. It isn't felt.

— ❦ —

It's better to kiss a miss than to miss a kiss.

Pete: I'll always remember her kisses—every time I open the refrigerator.

— 🍎 —

She prays every night: Dear Lord, I don't ask a thing for myself. Just send my parents a son-in-law.

— 🍎 —

When they kiss and make up, she gets the kiss and he the makeup.

— 🍎 —

It's done beneath the mistletoe,
    It's done beneath the rose.
But the proper place to kiss, you know,
    Is just beneath the nose.

— 🍎 —

"They do say," Mike began shyly, "that kisses are the language of love."
"Well, speak up," urged Linda.

— 🍎 —

A pretty girl forgot her fare,
    But the bus driver was not rough.
She kissed him sweetly then and there,
    And he said, "Fare enough."

He: If you refuse to kiss me, I'll hurl myself over that 500-foot cliff over there.

She: That's a lot of bluff.

— ❦ —

Boy: Ah, look at the cow and the calf rubbing noses in the pasture. That sight makes me want to do the same.

Girl: Well, go ahead—it's your cow.

— ❦ —

The young woman looked back to smile sweetly at the waiting line at the telephone booth. "I won't be long—I just want to hang up on him."

— ❦ —

Boy: Please whisper those three little words that will make me walk on air.

Girl: Go hang yourself.

— ❦ —

A boy becomes a man when he decides it's more fun to steal a kiss than second base.

— ❦ —

Sign in an airline's office: "God loves you, and I'm trying."

Husbands who kiss their wives every morning:

1. Live an average of five years longer.
2. Are involved in fewer automobile accidents.
3. Are ill 50% less time.
4. Earn 20–30% more money.

—West German newspaper

— 🦗 —

Kiss and hug, kiss and hug,
    Kiss your sweetie on the mug.

— 🦗 —

A kiss is the shortest distance between two.

— 🦗 —

A kiss is a contraction of the mouth due to an enlargement of the heart.

— 🦗 —

She: I'm telling you for the last time that I won't let you kiss me.
He: I knew you'd weaken.

— 🦗 —

Ted: Where did you get that black eye?
Red: For kissing the bride after the ceremony.
Ted: Isn't that the usual custom?
Red: But this was three years after the ceremony.

It's nice to kiss the kids goodnight—if you don't mind waiting up for them.

Sign at the New Orleans airport: "Start kissing good-bye early, so the plane can leave on time."

Kissing a girl in a canoe can be a very upsetting experience.

— 🍒 —

Sam: What's the difference between kissing your sister and your sweetheart?
Cam: About 25 seconds.

— 🍒 —

Girl: I always get weak when you kiss me, so I'm slapping you before you do.

— 🍒 —

Kissing is the anatomical juxtaposition of two orbicular muscles in the state of contraction.

— 🍒 —

He: So help me, I'll kiss you!
She: Kiss me, I'll help you.

— 🍒 —

A dean of women at a large coeducational college began an important announcement to the student body:
"The president of this college and I have decided to stop necking on this campus."
Met by a burst of laughter, the frustrated woman continued, "Furthermore, all the kissing that has been going on under my nose must be stopped."

Kiss and Tell

We have radio to thank for the information that love is "a matter of vitamin B-1, phosphorus and starch metabolism." During a WOR radio broadcast in New York, Dr. Carlton Fredericks was asked to explain the relationship between nutrition and kissing, and he told it—in full.

"When a fellow kisses a girl," said Dr. Fredericks, "the adrenosympathetic system calls on the liver for glycogen for energy. This in turn forces the release of insulin, vitamin B-1, and phosphorus to burn the sugar. In his brain, if he is doing any thinking, which is problematical, there is an exchange of starch, phosphorus, and thiamine between the thalamic and the cortical brain. As the pulse and respiration rates rise, there is increased exchange of oxygen on the intracellular level, which would mean increased consumption of thiamine and phosophorus."

A kiss is a noun, though often used as a conjunction; it is never declined; it is more common than proper, used in the plural and agrees with all genders.

— 🍎 —

He: Every time I kiss you it makes me a better man.

She: Well, you don't have to try to get to heaven in one night.

— 🍎 —

Kissing: A course of procedure, cunningly devised, for the mutual stoppage of speech at a moment when words are superfluous.

— 🍎 —

He: What would you take to give me a kiss?

She: Would you really like to know?

He: Yes!

She: Chloroform.

— 🍎 —

He: I just received a letter from my sweetheart and she put a couple of X's at the bottom of the letter. I sure am blue about it.

She: Why be blue about that?

He: Don't you know what the X's are for? They mean she's double-crossing me.

Todd: She said to me: "Stop! My lips are for another."

Rod: What did you say to that?

Todd: I said, "Well, if you'll hold still, you'll get another."

— ❦ —

I pressed my lips up to her cheek;
　　What could I do but linger,
And as my hand ran through her hair,
　　A cooty bit my finger.

— ❦ —

A kiss: Nothing divided by two; meaning persecution for the infant, ecstasy for the youth, fidelity for the middle-aged, and homage for the old.

— ❦ —

A kiss is a peculiar proposition. Of no use to one, yet absolute bliss for two. The small boy gets it for nothing, the young man has to ask for it, and the old man has to earn it. The baby's right, the lover's privilege, and the hypocrite's mask. To a young girl—faith; to a married woman—hope; and to an old maid—charity.

— ❦ —

Love at First Sight

First love: A little foolishness and a lot of curiosity.

—George Bernard Shaw

When it comes to falling in love, let the first impulse pass; wait for the second.

— 🍎 —

Many a man in love with a dimple makes the mistake of marrying the whole girl—Stephen Leacock.

— 🍎 —

There was a young girl from Iran
Who had trouble finding a man.
It was funny, you see,
Until she spotted me...
Then Iran and Iran and Iran.

— 🍎 —

Love at first sight is one of the greatest laborsaving devices the world has ever seen—Josh Billings.

First love: a little foolishness and a lot of curiosity—George Bernard Shaw.

The cure for love at first sight: second sight.

Courtship

Courtship—that period of time in which a man spends so much on his girlfriend that he finally decides to marry her for his money.

Courtship—a man pursuing a woman until she catches him.

— 🍎 —

You look at a potential husband the same way that you look at a house. You don't see it as it is, but as it will be after you get it remodeled.

— 🍎 —

Courtship—when a fellow gets so wrapped up in a girl that it's easy to tie the knot.

— 🍎 —

During courtship, the main influences of the moon are on the tide and the untied.

— 🍎 —

She's the kind of girl who likes to whisper sweet nothing-doings in his ear.

Newton's tenth law: the dimmer the porch light, the greater the scandle power.

— 🍎 —

Women are hard to figure out—the unmarried ones want to know if there's a man in their future, and the married ones want to know if there's a future in their man.

— 🍎 —

To lovers, even pockmarks look like dimples—Japanese proverb.

— 🍎 —

They gave each other a smile with a future in it—Lardner.

— 🍎 —

"I'm not wealthy, and I don't have a yacht and a convertible like Jerome Green," apologized the suitor. "But I love you."

"And I love you, too," replied the girl. "But tell me more about Jerome."

— 🍎 —

Jill: My pastor said we could have 16 husbands.

Jane: Are you sure about that?

Jill: Why, yes. At the last church wedding, I heard him say, "Four better, four worse, four richer, and four poorer!"

Marriage proposal: A speech usually made on the purr of the moment.

— ❦ —

A rich Texas student walked into a Cadillac showroom and told the salesman: "My girlfriend has a touch of the flu. What do you have in the way of a get-well car?"

— ❦ —

Student: Sir, what's a free thinker?
Professor: A free thinker is any man who isn't married.

— ❦ —

She shuts her eyes whenever we kiss,
    This maid so sweet and good.
And from my inmost heart I wish
    Her mother also would.

— ❦ —

Boy: Will you marry me?
Girl: No, but I'll always admire your good taste.

— ❦ —

Sam: My girlfriend takes advantage of me.
Pam: What do you mean?
Sam: I invited her to dinner and she asked me if she could bring a date.

"Do you have the book *Man, Master of Women*?" a young man asked the lady librarian.

"The fiction counter is to your left," the librarian replied.

Girl: Do you think you could be happy with a girl like me?

Boy: Perhaps, if she isn't too much like you.

— ❦ —

Courtship is that period when a girl strings a fellow along only to see if he's fit to be tied.

— ❦ —

Sign on steps of courthouse: "This way for marriage licenses. 'Watch your step!' "

— ❦ —

Sign on door of marriage license bureau: "Out to lunch. Think it over."

— ❦ —

Remember when boys used to chase girls? Now girls don't even run.

— ❦ —

It is better to be broke than to have never loved at all.

— ❦ —

Courtship—that period of time in which a man spends so much on his girlfriend that he finally decides to marry her for his money.

Mother: I don't believe Mary's boyfriend is what we thought he was.

Father: What's the trouble now?

Mother: He hung his hat over the keyhole.

— 🦋 —

She: I won't marry you until you have saved 1000 dollars.

After a year....

She: How much have you saved?

He: 35 dollars.

She: That's close enough.

— 🦋 —

John: Was that a new girl I saw you with last night?

Jack: No, just the old one painted over.

— 🦋 —

Pam: He was wonderful! Delightful! He said things to me no man has ever said.

Pat: What was that?

Pam: He asked me to marry him.

— 🦋 —

Tom: Since I met my new girl I can't eat, I can't sleep, I can't drink.

Tim: Why not?

Tom: I'm broke.

He: I would go to the end of the world for you!
She: Yes, but would you stay there?

— ❦ —

The surest way to hit a woman's heart is to take aim kneeling—Jerrold.

— ❦ —

She is a woman, therefore may be woo'd;
She is a woman, therefore may be won.
                                        —Shakespeare

— ❦ —

Faint heart never won fair lady.

— ❦ —

He who would the daughter win, must with the mother first begin.

— ❦ —

Woman begins by resisting man's advances and ends by blocking his retreat.

— ❦ —

She: Do you truly love me?
He: Very much, indeed.
She: Well, just how much?
He: Here's my checkbook. Just check the stubs.

Courtship makes a man spoon, but it's matrimony which makes him fork over.

— ❦ —

Lots of girls can be won for a song. Trouble is, it's the wedding march.

— ❦ —

Many a woman has started out playing with fire and has ended up cooking over it.

— ❦ —

"Four long years of college," sighed the girl graduate, "and who has it got me?"

— ❦ —

An unmarried girl is a like a baseball player—always trying to turn a single into a double.

— ❦ —

She didn't want to marry him for his money, but just couldn't figure out any other way to get it.

— ❦ —

Blonde to boyfriend at marriage license bureau: "Seems sort of silly to get a license after the hunting is over."

Advice to single gals: Don't go looking for the ideal man; a husband is much easier to find.

— 🐛 —

"When I was a single girl," she said reflectively, "I said I would never marry a man who was bald, wore glasses, or had artificial teeth. I didn't—but now he is, does, and has."

— 🐛 —

There are two ways of achieving success: by putting your shoulder to the wheel or putting your head on the shoulder of the man at the wheel.

— 🐛 —

Doris: When is your sister, Louise, thinking of getting married?
Little brother: Constantly!

— 🐛 —

Accidently meeting an acquaintance after several years, a girl said, "I never imagined you'd marry the man you did."
"Neither did I," replied the other. "I disliked his ways but adored his means."

— 🐛 —

"Darling, how can I ever leave you?"
"By bus, train, plane, or taxi."

He: Are you fond of nuts?
She: Is this a proposal?

What a wonderful night! The moon was out and so were his parents.

The playful, middle-aged wolf sidled up to the brunette. "Where have you been all my life?" he asked.

She looked at him coolly and replied, "Well for the first half of it, I wasn't born."

— ❦ —

"We're going to have a great time tonight," the boyfriend suggested. "I've got three tickets for the game."

"Why do we need three seats?" she asked.

"They're for your father, mother, and kid brother," he said.

— ❦ —

"Why is it that you go steady with that girl?"

"Well, because she's different from the other girls, I guess."

"How's that? In what way is she different?"

"She'll go with me."

— ❦ —

It's love when she sinks in his arms and ends up with her arms in the sink.

— ❦ —

At 20, a girl will ask: "Is he handsome?"

At 30, she asks: "Is he rich?"

At 35, she cries: "Where is he?"

"Will you love me when I'm old and gray?"
"Why must I wait that long?"

— ❦ —

"What makes you think they're engaged?"
"She has a ring and he's broke."

— ❦ —

Courtship, unlike proper punctuation, is a period before a sentence.

— ❦ —

Courtship is that part of a girl's life which comes between the lipstick and the broomstick.

— ❦ —

If men acted after marriage as they do during courtship, there would be fewer divorces—and more bankruptcies.

— ❦ —

Today young people start going steady with the opposite sex as soon as they learn there is one.

— ❦ —

Courtship—the only sport in which the person who gets caught has to buy the license.

Courtship—a love affair that begins like a violin with beautiful music, but ends with unconcern that the strings are still attached in marriage.

Before marriage a man yearns for a woman. After marriage, the "y" is silent.

Engagement

Engagement: In love, a period of occupation without possession.

The greatest salesman in the world is not a man—it's a girl selling her boyfriend the engagement ring.

— ❦ —

Engagement—the time the girl takes until she finds out if she can do any better.

— ❦ —

Engagement—a period of urge on the verge of merge.

— ❦ —

Engagement—a period in which a girl is placed in solitaire confinement.

— ❦ —

Teenage girl to friend: He hasn't proposed yet, but his voice has an engagement ring in it.

Charley: Tell me, dear, did any of your girlfriends notice your engagement ring?

Becky: Notice it? Two of them recognized it!

— ❦ —

Friend: You mean he asked you to give back all his presents?

Nurse (who had broken her engagement with her doctor boyfriend): Not only that, he sent me a bill for 55 visits.

— ❦ —

A diamond may not be as tight as a tourniquet, but it certainly stops the wearer's circulation.

— ❦ —

Coed to roommate: Sue was going to have an announcement party, but John broke the engagement. So she's letting the invitations stand and will just call it a "narrow-escape party"!

— ❦ —

Naturally, no one gives the groom a shower— he's all washed up, anyway.

— ❦ —

The first thing a girl hopes for from the garden of love is at least one carat.

She: Do you believe in long engagements?
He: Yes, the longer the better.

— ❦ —

In the bakery department of a Dallas supermarket, a wedding cake was set out for shoppers with the sign: "He changed his mind. Have a piece of cake on us."

Young typewriter salesman: Good morning. I came to your office about an attachment I have for your typewriter.

Clerk: Sorry, but she's out; and furthermore, she and I are engaged.

— ❦ —

June: I dislike people who are vague and noncommittal, don't you?

July: Mmmmmmmmmmmmmmmmmmmm.

— ❦ —

Candy: Look at my engagement ring.

Randy: That's a lovely ring. It's nice to know you're not marrying a spendthrift.

— ❦ —

She: If we become engaged, will you give me a ring?

He: Certainly, what's your number?

— ❦ —

He: Well, since you don't want to marry me after all, perhaps you'll return my ring.

She: If you must know, your jeweler has called for it already.

— ❦ —

Keep your eyes wide open before marriage and half shut afterwards—Franklin.

Pat: So you broke your engagement to Evelyn. Why was that?

Matt: Well, I was only doing to the engagement what it did to me.

— ❦ —

The little girl asked: "What makes a man always give a woman a diamond ring, Daddy?"

Replied Daddy: "The woman."

— ❦ —

The University of Tennessee's student newspaper column of engagements and weddings is titled "Who's Whose."

— ❦ —

A diamond is a woman's idea of a stepping-stone to success.

— ❦ —

Mac: My girlfriend said she'd be true to the end.

Cam: Well, what's wrong with that?

Mac: I'm a fullback.

— ❦ —

It takes two people to make a marriage: a single girl and a desperate mother.

He had been sitting with his girlfriend, Helga. An hour had gone by with no break in the silence in the parlor, when suddenly Olle blurted, "Helga, will you marry me?"

"Yes," answered Helga shyly.

Another hour of unbroken silence and Helga asked, "Olle, why don't you say something?"

To which Olle replied, "I tank I talk too much already."

"Sir," said the suitor, "I am seeking your daughter's hand."

"My boy," replied the father, "you can always find it in my pocket."

— ❦ —

"Dad," said the earnest young fellow, "I'm terribly in love with a beautiful girl. How can I find out what she really thinks of me?"

"Marry her, my boy. Marry her!"

— ❦ —

A marital expert says that when you see a man polishing a woman's car, you may be sure they are engaged; and when you see a woman polishing a man's car, you may be sure they are married.

— ❦ —

When a couple of young people start to eat onions, it's safe to pronounce them engaged.

— ❦ —

A woman might as well propose; her husband will claim she did.

— ❦ —

Pam: Bill told me I was the only girl he ever loved.

Pat: Doesn't he say it beautifully?

He: Here is your engagement ring.
She: But this diamond has a flaw in it.
He: You shouldn't notice that...we are in love and love is blind.
She: Not stone-blind.

— 🍂 —

Guy: Margie, I love you! I love you, Margie!
Gal: In the first place, you don't love me; and in the second place, my name isn't Margie.

— 🍂 —

She: If I refuse your engagement ring, will you really commit suicide?
He: That has been my usual procedure.

— 🍂 —

Stressing the importance of a large vocabulary, the English teacher told his class, "Use a word ten times, and it will be yours for life."

In the back of the room a pert blonde closed her eyes and was heard chanting under her breath, "Fred, Fred, Fred, Fred, Fred, Fred, Fred, Fred, Fred, Fred."

— 🍂 —

She: I'm sorry to disappoint you, but the fact is, last night I became engaged to Ernest.
He (knowing her): Well, how about next week?

He gave her a look that you could have poured on a waffle—Lardner.

— ❧ —

As Mark Twain said, "It's better to have old secondhand diamonds than none at all."

— ❧ —

Engagement: In love, a period of occupation without possession.

— ❧ —

My boyfriend just gave me a ring—it holds 20 keys.

— ❧ —

A girl who is expecting a ring will always answer the phone.

— ❧ —

Maude: The ring of sincerity was in his voice when he told me of his love.
May: It should have been in his hand. A ring in the hand is worth two in the voice.

— ❧ —

Diamond: one of the hardest substances known to man—especially to get back.

John: I suppose you've heard rumors I'm engaged to Peggy?

Jack: Yes. If it's true, I congratulate you; if not, I congratulate Peggy.

Larry: Broke your engagement to Mary?

Gary: She wouldn't have me.

Larry: You told her about your rich uncle?

Gary: She's my aunt now.

She: Oh, I wish the Lord had made me a man.

He: He did. I'm the man.

Weddings

There's nothing like a little exercise to change a man's life—especially if it's a walk down a church aisle.

Wedding ring—a one-man band.

— 🍎 —

Diamond jubilee—when the last installment is paid on the engagement ring.

— 🍎 —

Fran: Doesn't the bride look stunning?
Stan: Yes, and doesn't the groom look stunned?

— 🍎 —

Wedding—going over Niagara Falls without a barrel.

— 🍎 —

A father is a person who spends several thousand dollars on his daughter's wedding, then reads in the paper that he gave the bride away.

Wedding bells—a storm warning.

— ❦ —

Wedding vows might also include the phrase
" 'til debt do us part."

— ❦ —

A Hollywood wedding is one where they take
each other for better or worse—but not for long.

— ❦ —

Weddings have become so costly that it's now the
father of the bride who breaks down and weeps.

— ❦ —

Every bride has to learn it's not her wedding, but
her mother's—Lucy Johnson Nugent.

— ❦ —

A wedding usually means showers for the bride
and curtains for the groom.

— ❦ —

After paying for the wedding, about all a father
has left to give away is the bride.

— ❦ —

The best way for a bride to preserve her wedding
ring is to dip it in dishwater three times a day.

Wedding rehearsal—aisle trial.

— ❦ —

Father watching his daughter select the most expensive wedding gown: "I don't mind giving you away, but must I gift wrap you?"

— ❦ —

After the wedding: "They should be very happy. They're both so much in love with him."

— ❦ —

A wedding is a funeral where you smell your own flowers.

— ❦ —

Bride's father to groom: "My boy, you're the second-happiest man in the world."

— ❦ —

A wedding is proof that a man's willpower is no match for a girl with willpower.

— ❦ —

The worried bride-to-be told her mother that the most insignificant detail must not be overlooked at the wedding. "Don't worry," her mother replied, "he'll be there."

A wedding is a ceremony at which a man loses complete control of himself.

— ❦ —

Psychiatrists tell us that girls tend to marry men who are like their fathers. Now we know why mothers cry at weddings.

— ❦ —

The best and surest way to save a marriage from divorce is not to show up for the wedding.

— ❦ —

There's nothing like a little exercise to change a man's life—especially if it's a walk down a church aisle.

— ❦ —

Give a girl enough rope, and she'll ring the wedding bell.

— ❦ —

The most difficult years of marriage are those following the wedding.

— ❦ —

What is the bride thinking about as the organ plays the wedding march? "Aisle—Altar—Hymn."

Honeymoon

The cooing usually stops when the honeymoon is over, but the billing goes on forever.

The honeymoon is over when he phones that he'll be late for supper—and she's already left a note that it's in the refrigerator—Lawrence.

A honeymoon is a short period of doting between dating and debating.

Honeymoon—coo-existence.

A honeymoon is...
   —the thrill of a wife-time.
   —the period between "I do" and "You'd better."
   —the vacation a man takes before starting to work for a new boss.
   —the time during which the bride believes the bridegroom's word of honor.

The honeymoon is over when the dog brings your slippers and your wife barks at you.

— 🍎 —

You know the honeymoon is over when she complains about how much noise he makes while fixing his own breakfast.

— 🍎 —

The newlyweds were honeymooning in Florida. As they walked arm in arm along the beach, he looked out toward the sea and said in a most eloquent manner: "Roll on, thou deep and dark blue ocean, roll on."

His bride gazed at the breakers for a moment, then in hushed and reverent tones said: "Oh, Ralph, you wonderful man—it's doing it!"

— 🍎 —

The honeymoon is over when he no longer smiles gently as he scrapes the burnt toast.

— 🍎 —

The cooing usually stops when the honeymoon is over, but the billing goes on forever.

— 🍎 —

Honeymoon—the morning after the knot before.

There's nothing so unromantic as a seasick bride.

— ❦ —

The honeymoon is over when the bride begins to suspect that she was never anything to him but a tax deduction.

— ❦ —

The honeymoon is over when he finds out he married a big spender and she finds out she didn't.

— ❦ —

A honeymoon is the short period between the bridal toast and the burnt toast.

— ❦ —

The honeymoon is over when you realize that everything she says or cooks disagrees with you.

— ❦ —

The honeymoon is over when the wife stops making a fuss *over* her husband and begins to make a fuss *with* him.

— ❦ —

A woman in Arizona married so late in life that Medicare paid for her honeymoon.

Groom: What are you going to make for dinner?
Bride: Reservations.

— 🍎 —

Newlywed husband: Do you mean to say there's only one course for dinner tonight? Just cheese?
Bride: Yes, dear. You see, when the chops caught fire and fell into the dessert, I had to use the soup to put it out.

— 🍎 —

Newlywed couples shouldn't expect the first few meals to be perfect. After all, it takes time to find the right restaurant.

— 🍎 —

Honeymoon sandwich—just lettuce alone.

— 🍎 —

New bride bringing a dish to the social: The two things I prepare best are meatballs and peach pie.
Young man standing nearby: And which one is this?

— 🍎 —

Bride: Darling, you know that cake you asked me to bake for you? Well, the dog ate it.
Groom: That's okay, dear; don't cry. I'll buy you another dog.

Rookie husband: I've eaten so much frozen food that I have the only tonsils in town that are chapped.

— 🐛 —

Bride: I made this pudding all by myself.
Hubby: Splendid! But who helped you lift it out of the oven?

— 🐛 —

Husband: Beans again!
Wife: I don't understand it. You liked beans on Monday, Tuesday, and Wednesday, and now all of a sudden you don't like beans.

— 🐛 —

Groom: And here is an eggplant.
Bride: When will the eggs be ripe?

— 🐛 —

They were married for better or for worse. He couldn't have done better, and she could have done worse.

— 🐛 —

Marriage

Don't marry someone you can live with.
Marry someone you can't live without.
—Josh McDowell

Marriage is an educational institution in which a man loses his bachelor's degree without acquiring a master's.

— ❦ —

A man without a wife is but half a man.

— ❦ —

One wife defined marriage as "a give-and-take proposition." If her husband doesn't give her enough, she takes it out of his pocket.

— ❦ —

A successful marriage is one in which you fall in love many times, always with the same person—McLaughlin.

— ❦ —

Doing housework for 30 dollars a day is domestic service; doing it for nothing is matrimony.

I loved her then—I love her now—I love her now and then.

— ❦ —

Jane: I could have married anyone I please.
June: Then why are you single?
Jane: I never pleased anyone.

— ❦ —

Marriage is one long conversation checkered by disputes—Stevenson.

— ❦ —

Marriage has many pains, but celibacy has no pleasure—Johnson.

— ❦ —

Marry your son when you will, daughter when you can.

— ❦ —

Don't praise marriage on the third day, but after the third year.

— ❦ —

Often the difference between a successful marriage and a mediocre one consists of leaving about three or four things a day unsaid—Miller.

He who marries for wealth sells his liberty.

— ❦ —

The young man who wants to marry happily should pick out a good mother and marry one of her daughters—any one will do—Armour.

— ❦ —

No man is regular in his attendance at the House of Commons until he is married—Disraeli.

— ❦ —

If thee marries for money, thee surely will earn it—Ezra Bowen.

— ❦ —

The majority of husbands remind me of an orangutan trying to play the violin—Balzac.

— ❦ —

Marriage is three parts love and seven parts forgiveness of sins—Mitchell.

— ❦ —

One of the best hearing aids a man can have is an attentive wife—Groucho Marx.

Marriage at an Early Urge

Nice night
In June,
Stars shine,
Big moon;
On date,
With girl,
Heart pound,
Head swirl.

Happy girl,
Happy boy,
Me say,
Me love;
She coo
Like dove.

Me smart!
Me fast!
Never let
Chance pass;
"Get hitched,"
Me say,
She say,
"Okay!"

Wedding bells
Ring, ring
Honeymoon,
Everything.
Settle down,
Married life,
Happy man,
Happy wife.

Another night
In June,
Stars shine,
Big moon;
Ain't happy
No more.
Carry baby,
Walk floor,
Wife sad,
Me mad.

Life one
Big spat,
Nagging wife,
Bawling brat;
Me realize
At last,
Me too,
Too fast.

I'm the product of a mixed marriage—my father was a man and my mother was a woman.

It's too bad to see romance leave marriage. Sam's wife just sent him a twenty-fifth anniversary card addressed to Occupant.

Let there be spaces in your togetherness.

— ❧ —

Message to all brides: "If you should marry an archaeologist, you're in luck. The older you get, the more he will be interested in you."

— ❧ —

Don't marry someone you can live with. Marry someone you can't live without—Josh McDowell.

— ❧ —

As most veterans will tell you, marriage is the continuous process of getting used to things you hadn't expected.

— ❧ —

Marriage resembles a pair of shears, so joined that they cannot be separated; often moving in opposite directions, yet always punishing anyone who comes between them—Sydney Smith.

— ❧ —

Marriage is a long conversation which always seems too short—Maurois.

— ❧ —

The modern husband comes from work and greets his wife, "Hi, honey, what's thawing?"

"...and *then* I went to see the doctor—Maury, *Maury*!"

"Mmh?"

"Maury, are you listening to me or reading the newspaper?"

"I'm listening, I'm listening."

"I *said*, this afternoon I went to see Dr. Steinberg."

"Mmh." Maury turned the page. "So, how is he?"

A little common sense would prevent most divorces—marriages, too.

Marriage may often be a stormy lake, but celibacy is almost always a muddy horse-pond —Thomas Peacock.

There is one phase of life that I have never heard
    discussed in any seminar,
And that is that all women think men are funny
    and all men think that weminar.

—Ogden Nash

Confessing wife: My husband assures me that the way to hold a husband is not with expensive French perfume, but with the smell of freshly baked bread.

Sue: I suppose your husband is still taking it easy?

Jan: That's right. He only has two regrets in life. One is that he has to wake up to eat, and the other that he has to quit eating to sleep.

— ❧ —

George: My ambition is to marry a rich girl who is too proud to let her husband work.

— ❧ —

He acquired a large vocabulary—Tim got married.

— ❧ —

Tom: We're equal partners in our marriage. I'm the silent one.

— ❧ —

"Are you married?"
"No, I was hit by a truck."

— ❧ —

She: Darling, today we are married 12 months.
He: It seems more like a year to me.

— ❧ —

Marriages may be made in heaven, but a lot of the details have to be worked out here on earth.

Marriage would work out better if both sides would operate not only on the 50-50 basis but on the thrifty-thrifty basis as well.

— ❦ —

The story of some marriages should be told in a scrapbook.

— ❦ —

Men marry to make an end; women to make a beginning—A. Dupuy.

— ❦ —

Some pray to marry the man they love,
    My prayer will somewhat vary:
I humbly pray to Heaven above
    That I love the man I marry—Rose Stokes.

— ❦ —

"I wish," he said, "you could make pies like Mother used to bake."

"And I," said she, "wish that you made the dough Pa used to make!"

— ❦ —

When they asked the movie actress how long she had been married, she said, "This time, or all together?"

Love is a tie that binds; matrimony straps them together.

— ❦ —

Love makes marriage possible; habit makes it endurable.

— ❦ —

Marriage has many thorns, but celibacy has no roses.

— ❦ —

Marriage is a mutual partnership, in which either the husband or the wife can be the mute.

— ❦ —

Reality: After 20 awed years of married life, all troubles look smaller.

— ❦ —

Old-fashioned wife: one who tried to make one husband last a lifetime.

— ❦ —

It isn't long before a June husband forgets how to drive with one hand.

A woman should try to make her husband feel he is boss of the home, even if he's really just chairman of the fund-raising committee.

— ❦ —

Just about the time a woman thinks her work is all done, she becomes a grandmother.

— ❦ —

Try praising your wife—even if it does frighten her at first.

— ❦ —

If at first you don't succeed, do it the way your wife told you.

— ❦ —

The best way to remember your wife's birthday is to forget it once.

— ❦ —

Many couples are unhappily married, but fortunately don't know it.

— ❦ —

Two persons can now live as cheaply as a family of ten used to.

Frustrated wife to husband and children: Well, I worked out a budget, but one of us will have to go.

— 🐦 —

Jim: You say you never had a quarrel with your wife?

Tim: Never. She goes her way and I go hers.

— 🐦 —

"Who is your favorite author?"

"My husband."

"What does he write?"

"Checks."

— 🐦 —

Wife: You know, dear, you don't seem so well-dressed as you were when we were married ten years ago.

Husband: I don't know why not. I'm wearing the same suit.

— 🐦 —

The best way for a housewife to have a few minutes to herself at the close of the day is to start doing the dishes.

— 🐦 —

A judge asked a defendant why he struck his wife. The man replied, "Her back was turned, the broom was handy, and the back door was open."

After man came woman, and she has been after him ever since.

— ❦ —

Any man who has to ask for advice is probably not married.

— ❦ —

Fact: The argument you just won with your wife isn't over yet.

— ❦ —

After winning an argument with your wife, the wisest thing a man can do is apologize.

— ❦ —

The husband who boasts that he never made a mistake has a wife who did.

— ❦ —

Bigamy is having one wife too many—monogamy is often the same.

— ❦ —

If a child of God marries a child of the devil, the child of God is sure to have some trouble with his father-in-law.

Husbands are like wood fires. When unattended, they go out.

— 🍂 —

Love intoxicates a man; marriage often sobers him.

— 🍂 —

The most difficult years of marriage are those following the wedding.

— 🍂 —

The sanctity of marriage and the family relation make the cornerstone of our American society —James Garfield.

— 🍂 —

What therefore God hath joined together, let no man put asunder—Matthew 19:6 KJV.

— 🍂 —

Don't marry for money, you can borrow it cheaper—Scottish proverb.

— 🍂 —

Choose your wife, not at a dance, but in the harvest field—Czech proverb.

The ideal marriage is not one in which two people marry to be happy, but to make each other happy—Roy L. Smith.

— ❦ —

A fine wedding and the marriage license do not make the marriage; it is the union of two hearts that welds man and wife together.

— ❦ —

Sam: My wife and I have a joint checking account.
Cam: Isn't that hard to keep straight?
Sam: No, I put in the money, and she takes it out.

— ❦ —

Jim: Does your wife pick your clothes?
Tim: No, just the pockets.

— ❦ —

Before you run in double harness, look well to the horse.

— ❦ —

The average girl would rather have beauty than brains, because the average man can see better than he can think.

Whoso findeth a wife findeth a good thing, and obtaineth favour of the Lord—Proverbs 18:22 KJV.

— ❦ —

The only two who can live as cheaply as one are a flea and a dog.

— ❦ —

I call my wife Shasta. Shasta have this. Shasta have that.

— ❦ —

Herbert: My wife and I have a perfect understanding. I don't try to run her life, and I don't try to run mine either.

— ❦ —

Lillie: Your husband is lying unconscious in the hallway!
Millie: Goody, goody! My fur coat has come.

— ❦ —

Lou: How dare you burp before my wife?
Lon: I didn't know it was her turn.

— ❦ —

Will: It was a pleasure trip; I took my wife over to her mother's place.

Marriage occurs when a man gets caught on his own line.

— ❦ —

Marriage is called the Sea of Matrimony because it's so hard to keep your head above water.

— ❦ —

Marriage is like the army—everyone complains, but you'd be surprised at how many reenlist.

— ❦ —

Marriage is like a railroad sign—first you stop, then you look, then you listen.

— ❦ —

Marriage is an institution that turns a night owl into a homing pigeon.

— ❦ —

There are two things that cause unhappy marriages: men and women.

— ❦ —

A man is incomplete until he's married, and then he's finished.

Marriage is...

- the greatest adventure of all.
- a friendship recognized by the police —Stevenson.
- a public confession of a strictly private intention—Dayenhart.
- the thing that makes loving legal —Signoret.
- A souvenir of love—Rowland.
- an armed alliance against the world —Chesterton.
- all your money down and the rest of your life to pay.
- an institution that simplifies life and complicates living—Rostand.
- a period during which a man finds out what sort of fellow his wife would have preferred.
- working for nothing.
- the most expensive way to get your laundry done free—Charlie Jones.
- a romance in which the hero dies in the first chapter.
- a word that is not a word, but a sentence.
- the only game of chance the clergy favors.
- the only cure for love.
- the matrimonial high sea, for which a compass has yet to be invented.

Marriage is a process by which a grocer acquires an account the florist had—Rodman.

Back of every achievement is a proud wife and a surprised mother-in-law—Brooks Hays.

Marriage is a mistake every man should make—George Jessel.

Harry: I have half a mind to get married.
Larry: That's all you need.

— ❦ —

Being a husband is like any other job. It helps a lot if you like the boss.

— ❦ —

"I used to wake up a grouch," a wife confessed, "now I let him sleep."

— ❦ —

Joe: I just got a new car for my wife.
Roe: Now that's what I call a fair trade.

— ❦ —

"I suppose now that you are married you will be taking out some insurance?" the agent asked the bridegroom.

"Oh, no," he replied. "I don't think she's dangerous."

— ❦ —

Here lies my wife;
Here let her die!
Now she's at rest,
And so am I.
          —John Dryden
            epitaph

One husband's confession: My wife and I pledged we would never go to bed mad. Of course, we have gone without sleep for three weeks.

Wedlock, Not Deadlock

Seven "musts" for happy marriages:

1. Mutual Appreciation

2. Mutual Understanding

3. Mutual Fidelity

4. Mutual Responsibility

5. Mutual Respect

6. Mutual Faith

7. Mutual Love

What did I get married for?
　　That's what I want to know:
I was led to the altar
　　Like a lamb to the slaughter.

We met on Friday;
　　My luck was out, I'm sure:
I took her for better or worse, but she
　　Was worse than I took her for.

Fred: I hear you had an argument with your wife. How did it finally turn out?

Ted: Oh, she came crawling to me on her hands and knees.

Fred: No kidding! What did she say?

Ted: She said, "Come on out from under the bed, and fight like a man."

— ❦ —

Whenever my wife needs money, she calls me handsome. She says, "Hand some over."

— ❦ —

Housewarming—the last call for wedding presents.

— ❦ —

All husbands are alike, but they have different faces so you can tell them apart.

— ❦ —

I just heard of a man who met his wife at a travel bureau. She was looking for a vacation, and he was the last resort.

— ❦ —

Terry: Was your wife outspoken?

Harry: Not by anyone I know of.

This heartwarming ad appeared in the classified section of a dignified metropolitan paper:

"I am responsible for all debts and obligations of my wife, Julia, both present and future, and am delighted to be the provider for a woman who has borne me two fine children, listened patiently to all my gripes, and with an overabundance of love and care made the past 15 years of my life the happiest I have known. On this our fifteenth wedding anniversary, I am proud to express my gratitude publicly."

— ❦ —

There are only two ways to handle a woman, and nobody knows either of them.

— ❦ —

I heard a story about a man who had been married for over 30 years. Returning home from work one evening, he found his wife packing.

"What in the world are you doing?" he asked.

"I can't handle it anymore!" she cried. "We've done nothing but fight, argue, complain, and fuss at each other. I have decided to leave."

The man stood in shock and bewilderment as his wife walked out of the house—out of his life. Suddenly, he dashed into the bedroom and pulled down a suitcase from the closet shelf. Running outside, he yelled at his wife, "I can't handle it anymore either. Wait for me, and I will go with you."

Marry in haste, and repent at leisure.

Wife: Honey, I can't get the car started. I think it's flooded.
Husband: Where is it?
Wife: In the swimming pool.
Husband: It's flooded.

Wife: This is rabbit stew we're having.
Husband: Thought so. I just found a hair in mine.

— 🍎 —

Wife: I just got back from the beauty shop.
Husband: What was the matter? Was it closed?

— 🍎 —

Wife: I think you only married me because he left me a lot of money.
Husband: That's not true. I didn't care who gave you the money.

— 🍎 —

You don't know what you're missing, unless you've attended a modern Japanese wedding. Instead of rice, they throw transistor radios at the newlyweds.

— 🍎 —

Woman to marriage counselor: That's my side of the story—now let me tell you his.

— 🍎 —

Country cemetery stone epitaph: "Here lies my darling husband, Walter. May he rest in peace—until we meet again."

Bride to new husband: There you are, darling—my first meal cooked just the way you better like it.

— 🍎 —

Wife: My husband and I like the same things—but it took him 16 years to learn.

— 🍎 —

Husband: My wife talks to her plants for three hours every day. I once asked a geranium, "How do you stand it?"
It replied: "Who listens?"

— 🍎 —

I know a couple so concerned about their health that whenever they have an argument the wife jogs home to mother.

— 🍎 —

Adam was the luckiest man—he had no mother-in-law.

— 🍎 —

Punishment for bigamy: two mothers-in-law.

— 🍎 —

Ted: Your mother-in-law visited you only once?
Red: Yes, she came the day we were married and never left.

Mother-in-law:

- 🐦 a woman who seldom goes without saying.
- 🐦 a matrimonial kin who gets under your skin.
- 🐦 a person who often goes too far by being too near.
- 🐦 what you inherit free of charge when you marry your wife.
- 🐦 a puzzle full of cross words.
- 🐦 a woman who comes into the house voice first.

— 🐦 —

Tim: I heard your mother-in-law was dangerously ill last week.
Jim: Yes, but this week she's dangerously well again.

— 🐦 —

Think you've got troubles? My mother-in-law has a twin sister.

— 🐦 —

Be kind to your mother-in-law. Baby-sitters are expensive.

— 🐦 —

No man is really successful until his mother-in-law admits it.

What Is Love?

1. *Love is born of, or engenders respect.* There can be no real love where there is no respect.
2. *Love is surrender.* There is no domineering love.
3. *Love is emotion.* There is much that cannot be understood about love.
4. *Love is understanding.* It seeks to understand rather than criticize. It gives the benefit of the doubt where truth cannot be ascertained.
5. *Love is intelligent.* It is entered into with the whole being and should have the consent of the mind. "Puppy love" is all emotion; it has no balance and is not real.
6. *Love is reciprocal.* One-sided love cannot endure. Unrequited love is not normal. Love lives on love and grows by that which it lives on.
7. *Love is devoid of egotism.* One wrapped up in himself cannot properly appreciate or love another.
8. *True love cannot conceive of anything less than complete confidence.* Insofar as jealousy creeps in, love loses out.
9. *True love does not wear thin but grows and develops and deepens.*
10. *Love is consideration.* It seeks to determine and supply each desire of the other person. It should not need prodding.

Let us understand that it is not necessary that two persons be perfectly in love by the above standards before they marry. But let us surely ponder these and other definitions of love, that we may be sure that love is real before entering into a lifelong marriage bond.

After going steady for 12 years, we broke our engagement and got married.

— 🍎 —

The early part of our marriage was wonderful. The trouble started as we were leaving the church.

— 🍎 —

Love is never having to say you're sorry. Marriage is never having a chance to say anything.

— 🍎 —

Marriage is nature's way of keeping people from fighting with strangers!

— 🍎 —

Bill, affectionately to Valerie: Buttons keep my coat together, but you keep me warm inside.

— 🍎 —

One fellow said, "My wife is a very religious cook. Everything she serves is a burnt offering.

Adam and Eve

Adam and Eve had an ideal marriage. He didn't have to hear about all the men she could have married, and she didn't have to hear about the dishes his mother cooked.

Adam was born first—to give him a chance to say something.

— ❧ —

Q: At what time of day was Adam born?
A: A little before Eve.

— ❧ —

What a good thing Adam had going—when he said something, he knew nobody had said it before.

— ❧ —

Eve: Adam, do you love me?
Adam: Who else?

— ❧ —

The first Adam-splitting gave us Eve, a force which ingenious men in all ages have never gotten under control.

Teacher: Why was Adam a famous runner?
Student: Because he was the first in the human race.

It wasn't the apple on the tree but the pair on the ground that caused so much trouble in the garden.

Adam and Eve had an ideal marriage. He didn't have to hear about all the men she could have married, and she didn't have to hear about the dishes his mother cooked.

Whatever trouble Adam had,
    No man in days of yore
Could say when Adam cracked a joke—
    "I've heard that one before!"

Spinsters and Bachelors

Bachelor—A man whose wallet is full of near-Mrs.

Here lies the bones of Nancy Jones,
  For her life had no terrors,
She lived a maid and died a maid,
  No hits, no runs, no errors.

The girl who thinks no man is good enough for her may be right, but more often she is left.

Spinster—a woman who has been missed too long.

Spinster—a bachelor's wife.

Spinster—a woman who knows all the answers but no one has ever asked the question.

Mrs. Green: I've been looking for my husband for two hours.

Spinster: That's nothing, I've been looking for one for 20 years and haven't found him yet.

— ❦ —

Old maid—a lady in waiting.

— ❦ —

Old maid—girl with a wait problem.

— ❦ —

Bill: Why is Miss Jones wearing black?
Jill: She's in mourning for her husband.
Bill: Why, she never had a husband!
Jill: No, that is why she mourns.

— ❦ —

Did you hear about the desperate old maid who let dust accumulate under the bed because she heard that man is made out of dust?

— ❦ —

Janice: Husbands are such a worry.
Candice: Oh, I didn't know you had one.
Janice: I don't—that's what worries me.

A minister forgot the name of the couple he was to marry, so he said from the pulpit, "Will those wishing to be united in holy matrimony please come forward after the service?"

After the service, 13 old maids came forward.

Old maid's laughter—He! He! He!

Old maid—a woman without a gent to her name.

An old maid called the Fire Department: "A man is trying to get into my room."

"You don't want the Fire Department—you want the Police Department."

Old maid: "I don't want the police—I want the Fire Department. A man is trying to get into my room—and I'm on the second floor and he needs a ladder."

— 🍎 —

The prayer began, "Oh Lord, give us clean hearts, give us tender hearts, give us open hearts, give us sweet hearts," and every girl in the congregation silently but fervently responded, "Ah-men!"

— 🍎 —

Mrs. Brown (with newspaper): It says here that a woman in Kansas City has just cremated her third husband.

Miss Green: Oh my, isn't that just the way? Some of us can't get one and other women have husbands to burn.

— 🍎 —

Friend: Did you get any replies to your advertisement that a lonely maiden sought light and warmth in her life?

Spinster: Yes, two from electric light companies and one from the gas company.

A bachelor is a man...

- who thinks before he acts, and then doesn't act.

- who never Mrs. anyone.

- who enjoys the chase, but does not eat the game.

- who leans toward women, but not far enough to lose his balance.

- who is completely dedicated to life, liberty, and the happiness of pursuit.

- who takes advantage of the fact that marriage is not compulsory.

- who never makes the same mistake once.

- who has no children to speak of.

- who is crazy to get married, and realizes it.

- who sees no sense in losing his best friend by marrying her.

- who knows there are two kinds of men: the quick and the wed.

- who has un-altar-able views.

- who can only be miss-led so far.

- who steers clear of women with bride ideas.

- who has never met a woman he couldn't live without.

- who believes all wives dress to kill—and cook the same way.

- who avoids tying a knot around a woman's finger for fear of ending up under her thumb.

- ❧ who won't take a wife to share his life because he knows that shareholders often become directors.

- ❧ whose wallet is full of near-Mrs.

- ❧ who would rather be on the outside looking in than on the inside looking out.

- ❧ who looks before he lips.

- ❧ whose agility gives him an arrow escape from Cupid.

- ❧ who prefers to cook his own goose.

- ❧ who thinks that the only thoroughly justified marriage was the one that produced him.

- ❧ who believes it is much better to have loved and lost than to have to get up for the 2 A.M. feeding.

- ❧ who lost the opportunity of making some woman miserable.

- ❧ who is footloose and fiancée free.

- ❧ who is a souvenir of some woman who found a better one at the last moment.

- ❧ who can have a girl on his knee without having her on his hands.

- ❧ who can go fishing anytime, until he gets hooked.

- ❧ who can't be spouse-broken.

- ❧ who is allergic to wedding cake.

- ❧ who is footloose and family-free.

- who knows how to hold a woman's hand so she doesn't get a grip on him.
- who makes mistakes, but not in front of the preacher.
- who never chases a woman he couldn't outrun.
- who plays the game of love and manages to keep his amateur standing.
- who washes one set of dishes.
- who won't take yes for an answer.
- who would rather change girls than change their names.

— 🕭 —

A man who refused to fight used to be called a coward. Now they call him a bachelor.

— 🕭 —

For a man to remain a bachelor calls for a cool head—or cold feet!

— 🕭 —

Not all men are fools. Some are bachelors.

— 🕭 —

"Is it true, Miss Elderleigh, that you are going to be married soon?"

"Well, no, it isn't. But I am very grateful for the rumor."

Neighbor: You can get anything from a mail-order house.

Spinster: Everything, alas, but a male.

Abner Jones loved Sally Johnson, a spinster, but never had courage enough to propose, being invariably overwhelmed with shyness when he met her. At last, he determined to put his fate to the test and phoned her.

"Miss Johnson?"

"Miss Johnson speaking."

"Er—will you marry me, Miss Johnson?"

"Yes! Who is speaking?"

— 🐛 —

The spinster pooh-poohed anyone who suggested that it was too bad she did not have a husband.

"I have a dog that growls, a parrot that swears, a fireplace that smokes, and a cat that stays out all night. Why should I want a husband?"

— 🐛 —

Helen: How is your bachelor friend?

Kevin: When I saw him last he was mending slowly.

Helen: Why, I didn't know he'd been ill.

Kevin: He hasn't been. He was sewing buttons on his clothes.

— 🐛 —

Optimistic bachelor: Let's get married!

Pessimistic spinster: Good heavens! Who'd have us?

— 🐛 —

Divorce

There would be fewer divorces if the husband tried as hard to keep his wife as he did to win her.

The three chief causes of divorce are men, women, and marriage.

Love is the quest, marriage the conquest, divorce the inquest.

A divorce is what couples agree on when they can't agree on anything else.

Judging by the divorce rate, a lot of people who said "I do"—didn't.

A man and his wife were divorced because of illness—they got sick of each other.

Divorce is hash made of domestic scraps.

— 🍎 —

Divorce occurs when you'd rather switch than fight.

— 🍎 —

There would be fewer divorces if the husband tried as hard to keep his wife as he did to win her.

— 🍎 —

Desertion is the poor man's method of divorce.

— 🍎 —

Love at first sight usually ends with divorce at first slight.

— 🍎 —

The worst reconciliation is better than the best divorce—Cervantes.

— 🍎 —

A modern miracle would be a golden wedding anniversary in Hollywood.

 — 🍎 —

Alimony

Alimony—Bounty on the mutiny.

There are only two ways to avoid alimony: either stay single or stay married.

— —

Paying alimony is like paying installments on a car after you've wrecked it.

— —

Alimony is a system in which one pays for the mistakes of two.

— —

You never know how short a month is until you pay alimony.

— —

Alimony—a man's transition from a costarring spot to a supporting role.

Alimony is like buying oats for a dead horse.

Alimony is payment for services not rendered.

Alimony is...

- 🍎 the billing without the cooing.
- 🍎 bounty on the mutiny.
- 🍎 giving comfort to the enemy.
- 🍎 the matrimonial institution's severance pay.
- 🍎 a husband's cash-surrender value.
- 🍎 a pay-as-you-go plan.
- 🍎 taxation without representation.
- 🍎 a matter of wife and debt.
- 🍎 heart-earned money.
- 🍎 the take from a mistake.
- 🍎 a war debt.
- 🍎 a wife's guaranteed annual wage.
- 🍎 matrimony's price of peace.
- 🍎 the wages of sin.

Senior Love

The heart that loves is always young.

An old man in love is like a flower in winter
—Portuguese proverb.

— ❦ —

Love at first sight is easy to understand; it's when
two people have been looking at each other for a
lifetime that it becomes a miracle—Levinson.

— ❦ —

You're retired when you don't care where your
wife goes, just as long as you don't have to go along.

— ❦ —

In the window of a Kansas City beauty salon:
"We can give you the new look—if you have the old
parts."

— ❦ —

Over a stack of secondhand casings in a Detroit
gas station: "Experienced tires for sale."

She suddenly had an urge to live in the past and said, "You used to kiss me." So he leaned over and kissed her. "You used to hold my hand," she said. So he reached out and held her hand. "You used to bite me on the back of the neck," she added. He got up and walked out of the room.

"Where are you going?"

"To get my teeth."

— ❦ —

On the rear of a 1931 automobile as it crawled along a Tampa, Florida street: "Don't laugh. Remember, you'll be old someday, too."

— ❦ —

Age is a matter of mind. If you don't mind, it doesn't matter.

— ❦ —

I like my bifocals,
    My dentures fit me fine,
My hearing aid is perfect,
    But how I miss my mind!

— ❦ —

You aren't fully dressed 'til you put on a smile.

— ❦ —

Growing older is a journey from passion to compassion.

Two retirees were "cooling it" in a small-town jail, following a sentence for fishing out of season.

First fisherman: That's really a stiff sentence, and we did have our licenses!

Second fisherman: Don't worry, we'll be out in no time. My wife hasn't let me finish a sentence in 40 years.

Don't take life too seriously—you'll never get out of it alive.

— 🍎 —

Sign in a Florida convenience store: "Call home now! Save a trip! Forget anything?"

— 🍎 —

I'll never make the mistake of being 70 again— Casey Stengel.

— 🍎 —

Will Rogers said, "We are all here for a spell; get all the good laughs you can."

— 🍎 —

He who cries over spilled milk should condense it.

— 🍎 —

Leisure time is when your wife can't find you.

— 🍎 —

The heart that loves is always young.

— 🍎 —

If I'd known I was going to live so long, I'd have taken better care of myself—Eubie Blake.

Go ahead and touch me; wrinkles aren't contagious.

— 🍒 —

When your memory goes, forget it!

— 🍒 —

The first thing I do in the morning is breathe on the mirror and hope it fogs up—Early Wynn.

— 🍒 —

Love's like the measles: all the worse when it comes late in life—Jerrold.

— 🍒 —

A man is as old as he feels; a woman is as old as she looks.

— 🍒 —

Grandparents never say, "We'll have to see about it later!" They do it now!

— 🍒 —

Grandmothers need more hugs than mothers.

Other Good
Harvest House Reading

PROVERBS FOR PEOPLE
by *Vern McLellan*

Clever proverbs are matched with a corresponding
Scripture reference and illustration that will bring
a smile and a cause for reflection with the turn of
each page.

PROVERBS, PROMISES, AND PRINCIPLES
by *Vern McLellan*

A stimulating new collection of thought-provoking
sayings and colorful anecdotes to give your life and
conversation a lift. Contains hundreds of new topics
handled in a skillful and readable style. By the
author of *Quips, Quotes, and Quests*.

QUIPS, QUOTES, AND QUESTS
by *Vern McLellan*

You will never be without a wise or witty saying
after you read *Quips, Quotes, and Quests*. This
compilation of famous (and infamous) Bible verses,
quotations, and sayings is a handy reference for the
whole family.

WIT AND WISDOM
by *Charlie "T" Jones* and *Bob Phillips*

Bestselling humorist Bob Phillips combines his
talent with the unforgettable Charlie
"Tremendous" Jones and takes you through the
alphabet laughing all the way.

WISE WORDS FROM A WISE GUY
by *Vern McLellan*

Back with his latest collection of the wise and
wacky, master wordsmith Vern McLellan is ready to
brighten your life and conversation with illustrated
principles and humor based on the sayings of
Solomon and others.

Filled with a multitude of conversation-starters,
quick comebacks, and inspirational morsels
delightfully illustrated by Sandy Silverthorne, *Wise
Words from a Wise Guy* is a perfect gift—for yourself
or a friend—with a wisdom-filled message!

ALL AMERICAN JOKE BOOK
by *Bob Phillips*

A riotous, fun-filled collection of over 800
anecdotes, puns, and jokes.

IN SEARCH OF BIBLE TRIVIA—Vol. 1
by *Bob Phillips*

A stimulating collection of well-known and little-
known Bible facts from bestselling author Bob
Phillips. Don't miss this opportunity to test your
Bible knowledge.

IN SEARCH OF BIBLE TRIVIA—Vol. 2
by *Bob Phillips*

Volume 2 comes with more than 700 all-new
questions and answers. Inspiring and educational, it
will increase your Bible knowledge and
understanding.

Dear Reader:

We would appreciate hearing from you regarding this Harvest House fiction book. It will enable us to continue to give you the best in Christian publishing.

1. What most influenced you to purchase *Love Lines*?
   - ☐ Author
   - ☐ Subject matter
   - ☐ Backcover copy
   - ☐ Recommendations
   - ☐ Cover/Title
   - ☐ _____

2. Where did you purchase this book?
   - ☐ Christian bookstore
   - ☐ General bookstore
   - ☐ Department store
   - ☐ Grocery store
   - ☐ Other

3. Your overall rating of this book:
   - ☐ Excellent
   - ☐ Very Good
   - ☐ Good
   - ☐ Fair
   - ☐ Poor

4. How likely would you be to purchase other books by this author?
   - ☐ Very likely
   - ☐ Somewhat likely
   - ☐ Not very likely
   - ☐ Not at all

5. What types of books most interest you? (check all that apply)
   - ☐ Women's Books
   - ☐ Marriage Books
   - ☐ Current Issues
   - ☐ Self Help/Psychology
   - ☐ Bible Studies
   - ☐ Fiction
   - ☐ Biographies
   - ☐ Children's Books
   - ☐ Youth Books
   - ☐ Other _____

6. Please check the box next to your age group.
   - ☐ Under 18
   - ☐ 18-24
   - ☐ 25-34
   - ☐ 35-44
   - ☐ 45-54
   - ☐ 55 and over

Mail to: Editorial Director
Harvest House Publishers
1075 Arrowsmith
Eugene, OR 97402

Name _____

Address _____

City _____ State _____ Zip _____

**Thank you for helping us to help you
in future publications!**